D1154295

Children of the World
Ireland

For a free color catalog describing Gareth Stevens' list of high-quality books, call 1-800-341-3569 (USA) or 1-800-461-9120 (Canada).

For their help in the preparation of *Children of the World: Ireland*, the writer would like to thank Dennis Regan for helping to locate an Irish family for this book, Mary Kruser for introducing her wonderful Irish relatives, Nora and Oliver Healy and all their helpful and hospitable relatives, and Brother Daley and the faculty of the Christian Brothers Day School for their generous cooperation. The warmth and good wishes of all these loving Irish people transformed the making of this book into a delightful adventure. The editor would also like to gratefully thank Professor John Gleeson of the University of Wisconsin - Milwaukee.

Library of Congress Cataloging-in-Publication Data

Holland, Gini.
    Ireland / by Gini Holland.
        p.   cm. — (Children of the world)
    Includes index.
    Summary: Presents the life of an eleven-year-old boy and his family in Ireland, describing his home and school activities and discussing the history, geography, people, government, economy, and culture of his country.
        ISBN 0-8368-0246-2
    I. Ireland—Juvenile literature. [I. Ireland.] I. Title. II. Series.
    DA906.H65   1991
    941.5—dc20   89-43187

Edited, designed, and produced by
Gareth Stevens Publishing
1555 North RiverCenter Drive, Suite 201
Milwaukee, Wisconsin 53212, USA

Series editor: Valerie Weber
Editor: Patricia Lantier-Sampon
Research editor: John D. Rateliff
Designer: Sharone Burris
Map design: Sheri Gibbs

Printed in the United States of America

1 2 3 4 5 6 7 8 9 98 97 96 95 94 93 92

Children of the World
Ireland

Text and Photography by Gini Holland

Gareth Stevens Publishing
MILWAUKEE

. . . a note about *Children of the World*:

The children of the world live in fishing towns, Arctic regions, and urban centers, on islands and in mountain valleys, on sheep ranches and fruit farms. This series follows one child in each country through the pattern of his or her life. Candid photographs show the children with their families, at school, at play, and in their communities. The text describes the dreams of the children and, often through their own words, tells how they see themselves and their lives.

Each book also explores events that are unique to the country in which the child lives, including festivals, religious ceremonies, and national holidays. The *Children of the World* series does more than tell about foreign countries. It introduces the children of each country and shows readers what it is like to be a child in that country.

Children of the World includes the following published and to-be-published titles:

Afghanistan	El Salvador	Jordan	Saudi Arabia
Argentina	England	Kenya	Singapore
Australia	Finland	Malaysia	South Africa
Austria	France	Mexico	South Korea
Belize	Greece	Morocco	Spain
Bhutan	Guatemala	Nepal	Sweden
Bolivia	Honduras	New Zealand	Tanzania
Brazil	Hong Kong	Nicaragua	Thailand
Burma (Myanmar)	Hungary	Nigeria	Turkey
Canada	India	Norway	USSR
China	Indonesia	Panama	Vietnam
Costa Rica	Ireland	Peru	West Germany
Cuba	Israel	Philippines	Yugoslavia
Czechoslovakia	Italy	Poland	Zambia
Denmark	Jamaica	Portugal	
Egypt	Japan	Romania	

. . . and about *Ireland*:

Eleven-year-old Brian lives in the small village of Puckane with his parents and his sister, Siobhan. Brian works hard at developing his mind as well as his body; he studies hard at school and plays several instruments. But nothing beats the excitement of playing the Irish game of hurling, which Brian practices as often as possible with friends and relatives.

To enhance this book's value in libraries and classrooms, comprehensive reference sections include current information about Ireland's geography, demographics, language, currency, education, culture, industry, and natural resources. *Ireland* also features a bibliography, glossaries, research topics, activity projects, and discussions of such subjects as Dublin, the country's history, language, political system, and ethnic and religious composition.

The living conditions and experiences of children in Ireland vary according to economic, environmental, and ethnic circumstances. The reference sections help bring to life for young readers the rich excitement of Ireland's culture and heritage. Of particular interest are discussions of Ireland's efforts to maintain peace in spite of religious and political turmoil and its fierce determination to preserve its colorful Gaelic traditions.

CONTENTS

Above: Brian, with his parents, Mary and Tony, and his sister, Siobhan, watches boaters from the banks of Lough Derg.

Inset: Brian Lawlor of Puckane, Ireland.

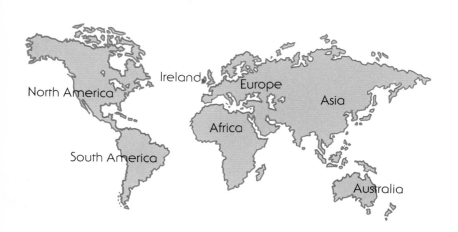

LIVING IN IRELAND:
Brian, a Young Athlete and Musician

Brian Lawlor is 11 years old and lives with his sister, Siobhan, and his parents, Mary and Tony, outside the tiny Irish town of Puckane in south-eastern Ireland. Brian's home in County Tipperary is an old country house on the narrow road to Puckane and is surrounded by farmland that used to belong to his father's parents. Brian's father planted a line of trees alongside the gravel drive and made a flower garden there as well, but he left plenty of room for Brian to practice his favorite Irish sport of hurling on the flat lawn beside the house.

Behind the Lawlor house stands a barn where Brian's grandparents used to keep livestock. Now only chickens and two ducks that Siobhan named Sam and Winnie live there. Siobhan hopes their eggs will hatch into ducklings.

The old family brick barn, now empty, still stands behind Brian's home. The barn is a reminder of Grandfather Lawlor's farming days.

A Walk through Brian's Country Town of Puckane

The town of Puckane (Puh-KAHN) is very small. Brian can walk along the narrow two-lane road that leads from his house to the town in about 15 minutes. It only takes another ten minutes on that same road to walk through the town of Puckane. Then he is out in the country again. Trees on either side of the road reach their branches in an arch over the highway, so Brian feels like he's walking in a tunnel that is green with leaves and noisy with the sounds of birds.

Irish windows celebrate the gentle island climate with flowers.

An old-fashioned thatched roof keeps this Puckane cottage dry and well insulated.

Like most places in Ireland, the town of Puckane spells its name in both Gaelic (Irish) and English so that the old Gaelic language of Ireland will not be forgotten.

Puckane has several small businesses, a church, dairies, two taverns, a hotel with a restaurant, and thatched cottages for tourists to rent. The road behind the church leads to the football field, where the boys in town practice Gaelic football. The team's clubhouse stands on one side of the field, and new houses appear only a short distance away. But sheep are still the main spectators when Brian's team practices.

Neighboring Farmland Is a Playground

Brian's aunt and uncle live in the house next door, so his cousins run in and out of his house all day long, playing games with him and Siobhan. It's fun to have cousins for neighbors, even if they are younger. On rainy days, everyone likes to play video games on the television monitor Brian has in his bedroom. When they watch television programs, they go into the sitting room.

But on sunny days, everyone prefers to play outside on the neighboring farmland. The grassy hill behind Brian's house is perfect for flying kites because there are no trees. When the wind blows steadily, Brian and his cousins can get a kite to go so high it almost disappears.

Brian lets Siobhan have a turn at his newest video game.

Brian's father has created flower gardens in front of the house that still leave plenty of space for the children to play.

Brian loves sports and often gets his cousins to help him practice Irish hurling. Siobhan doesn't hurl, but she is happy to join a game of volleyball. They tie a rope between two trees and use a giant beach ball with a map of the world on it. When they hit the ball really hard, it looks like the earth is going into a new orbit.

Brian's hurling sticks and tennis equipment have to wait until homework is complete.

Nenagh — A Lively, Prosperous Fairground

Nenagh, the town where Brian and Siobhan attend school, means "Fair Ground" in Gaelic, or Irish. English is an official primary language of Ireland, but Gaelic is still used as well on all street signs and public announcements. Brian and Siobhan study Gaelic in school daily, learning to read and write the language of their ancestors. But in daily life, they speak English.

Nenagh is a prosperous community with shops and tearooms for local citizens and tourists. Some big tourist attractions are the 13th-century Nenagh Castle and the old Governor's House and Gatehouse that once held the county jail.

Nenagh Castle. Thirteenth-century castles had lots of narrow windows and spaces around the top so that archers could shoot arrows to defend the building and still hide from enemies.

Bicycles are a favorite way to get around town for young and old alike. In this picture, a bike is propped up, unlocked, against the old Healy butcher shop in Nenagh.

Before he retired, Brian's grandfather helped start a butcher shop in Nenagh. Brian's mother shops for meat at her father's old shop, which still has his name above the door. She does the rest of her shopping at the supermarket. Her father also started the large meat-packing company, the Anglo-Irish Beef Processors, where she now works. This company and the silver mines outside of town are the largest employers in the area.

Busy Times with Cars and Computers

Brian's parents do not farm as his grandparents on his father's side once did. Brian's father delivers new cars for a local car dealership, called Slattery's, which is just off the road outside of Puckane. When Brian sees a shiny new car in their driveway, he knows his father has stopped home for a moment before delivering the car. Sometimes his father drives as far as Dublin; other times he delivers cars to nearby towns.

Brian's mother works in the office of the Anglo-Irish Beef Processors. She has her own desk and spends much of her day at the computer, working with the accounts. Farmers from all around Nenagh bring their cattle and sheep to be slaughtered and processed here. When she started, Brian's mother worked in the meat-processing plant, making sausage. But she prefers working in the office with the other accountants and secretaries. It's cleaner and much quieter.

Brian's house has been in his father's family for a long time. After Brian's grandparents died, Tony, Brian's father, sold the surrounding farmland, preferring not to farm. Today, Tony is driving his employer's van.

Brian's mother, Mary, works five days a week while her children are in school. ▶

14

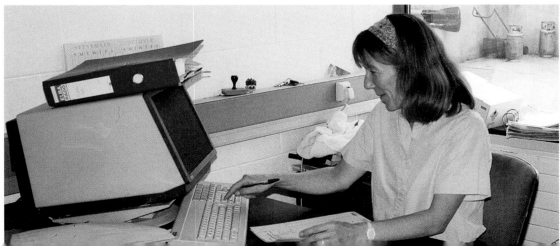

15

Schooltime in Nenagh

Puckane has a small school, but Brian and Siobhan go to school in Nenagh. So every weekday from September to June, Brian's mother drives Brian and Siobhan to school on her way to work. Irish schools are funded by the government but run by religious organizations. Most schools are separated into boys' schools and girls' schools, where all students wear uniforms. The Christian Brothers run Brian's school, and Siobhan goes to St. Mary's Convent School, where her mother and grandmother went before her. There are also smaller Protestant schools in Nenagh.

Brian and his schoolmates play outside before the morning bell, exchanging stories of hurling and football matches and after-school plans. They set their lunch boxes on a shelf built against a wall of an outdoor shelter. The shelter is lined with benches to sit on in good weather. Then Brian and his friend Michael go inside early to set up the computers for the classrooms that need them.

In the morning mist, the older boys walk around Brian's school building to the Christian Brothers high school. The playing fields on their right should be dry in time for afternoon athletic practice.

These young lads enjoy playing a game of hurling together when their school lessons are done.

The boys store their lunches out of the sun in this shelter near the side of the school yard.

Preparing for the first bell, the boys line up by class. Uniforms, including the school tie, are required, but jackets and bookbags can be any color, any style.

A good student, Brian carefully answers questions from his Gaelic language book.

Mr. O'Brien runs an efficient classroom, listening to a student read while he has another boy erase the board in time for the next example.

When the bell rings, the rest of the boys line up and change from noisy sportsmen to serious students. They enter class and quickly find their seats, sitting in pairs at their desks. They like their teacher, Mr. O'Brien, because he relates their studies to sports and events in daily life and keeps things going at a good pace. He starts out the day with a number on the board and asks them to tell him all the ways they can think about that number. The boys all raise their hands crying "Sir! Sir!" and the discussion is off and running.

In addition to math, the boys study English and geography before lunch. They keep their books and supplies ready in their schoolbags so they can quickly get them out when Mr. O'Brien asks for written work or wants them to read. Anyone caught not paying attention must stand in place for a minute to "wake up." This usually keeps the boys from daydreaming. They never know when their teacher is going to call on them, so they try to pay attention.

Music and *A Touch of Class*

After lunch, Brian and three of his friends come back inside to practice music. They are starting a rock band for which Brian plays the keyboard while his friends sing and play the accordion and drums. They are working to become good enough so they can play for school and local dances.

After practice, the boys study science and Irish language and culture until it's time for physical education. Then they get ready for the Nenagh Christian Brothers School Band. The school band is very successful, and Brian is proud to be one of its accordion players. All members wear red ties, long black capes with red linings, and hats to match. Brother Daley, the school principal, directs the band and manages everything from music to making sure each boy finds a cape that fits. The band has made several records of its music. The latest one is called *A Touch of Class*.

◀ All the boys in Brian's class try to participate in class discussions.

Below: The Nenagh Christian Brothers School Band proudly shows off its uniforms.

Football Practice = Hard Work

Compared to the games Brian plays at home, Gaelic football practice is serious business. After school, the boys drop off their gear bags outside the clubhouse. Their coach separates them into two teams, tells them what positions to play, and gets them started. It takes strength and skill to play a good game of football. Brian is fast and energetic, and the coach relies on him to break through any defense the other boys might set up.

To get selected for a position on the team, each boy raises his hand and cries "Sir! Sir! Sir!" until he is chosen.

Above: Brian and the ball are airborne in this fast-moving play.

Right: Brian's mother and sister are impressed with Brian's skill on the football field.

By the end of an hour, some boys are so winded they have to lie in the grass to catch their breath. But most are strong from daily practice. The coach talks to them about strategy and jumps in the air to show how to get the ball away from an opposing team. When Brian's mother and Siobhan come to watch the team practice, they follow Brian carefully as he plays skillfully with his teammates.

Siobhan's All-Girls' School and Irish Dancing

At Siobhan's school, all the girls wear gray wool jumpers and yellow blouses. They wait on the playground for the morning bell to ring while Sister Stephania, the school principal, energetically sweeps the steps. Some girls have brought flowers for their teachers and hold them patiently until the bell rings for them to go inside.

In class, Siobhan's teacher puts lessons on the board. She asks the girls to raise their hands quietly if they wish to speak.

As at Brian's school, the girls at Siobhan's school must wear the same uniform, but their school bags can be any style.

Once a week after school, Siobhan walks the few blocks to dance class. She enjoys practicing with her Irish dance teacher, who helps her learn the different steps and smiles even when Siobhan doesn't get them right the first time.

After class, Siobhan's mother picks her up and drives to her aunt's house, where Brian is waiting for them. Then they all drive back to Puckane. If Brian and Siobhan are good, they stop for a treat of "crisps," or potato chips, to make the wait until dinnertime a little easier.

When she learns a new dance step, Siobhan practices carefully until she gets it right.

25

Country Castles to Climb

Castle ruins stand all over Ireland, and many towns have ancient castle walls and parts of towers and great halls running right through their center. Every day on the way to school, Brian and Siobhan pass an old castle tower in the middle of a field near their house. Nothing but cow pastures and woods are around it now, but it is easy to imagine medieval knights, lords, and ladies climbing up this tower for a view of the countryside around Puckane.

Another building unique to these Irish country towns is the doctor's clinic. Since it is such a small town, the doctor only comes to Puckane's clinic twice a week. If someone needs a doctor at another time, they must drive into the town of Nenagh.

In addition to providing weekly visits by a doctor and a midwife, this country dispensary outside Puckane records births, deaths, and marriages.

◀ Gradually crumbling away in the wind, this section is all that remains of an old castle tower just outside of Puckane.

◀ Inset: On summer days, Brian and Siobhan can explore ancient ruins.

27

Cousin Lily blows out two candles for her second birthday, while Siobhan and her cousins encourage her.

Nenagh Cousins at Baby Lily's Birthday Party

Brian and Siobhan get to see their cousins in Nenagh every day after school. Except for dancing lessons or football practices, they stay with their Aunt Ann until their mother gets off of work and can drive them back to Puckane. Today it's baby Lily's birthday, and Aunt Ann has made a cake for the occasion. Brian prefers to go swimming at the local pool, but Siobhan stays for the party.

Their little cousins are so silly! They pass a piece of cake around and around the table, too full to eat another bite. Then they decide to make music and dance with one another like the grown-ups do.

Siobhan convinces them it would be more fun to make a play and use the window seat as a stage. Soon they are all in capes and costumes, coming in and out of the window to make their hilarious stage show.

At baby Lily's party, imagination is the best ingredient for a fun-filled afternoon.

Brian's Father Lends a Hand

When Brian builds or fixes something, his father is glad to work with him. They can repair broken toys, put a kite together quickly, or make something new. When Brian's new video game stopped working, his father helped him discover what was wrong. They unscrewed the case to the electrical converter and found that Brian and his friends had played with the game so much they had burned the wiring inside. Brian's father drove into Nenagh for a new converter. Brian was glad that his father could help him discover the problem and help make it right again.

When Brian's father sits back to read the paper, he sometimes reads articles to Brian and Siobhan about world events and asks their opinion about the issues. When he reads about wars, Brian says, "It's a big waste when the money could be going to starving countries." He hopes that people learn to settle their differences peacefully so that he and Siobhan can grow up in a world that is safe for all living things.

When something mechanical breaks, Brian can count on his dad to help with repairs.

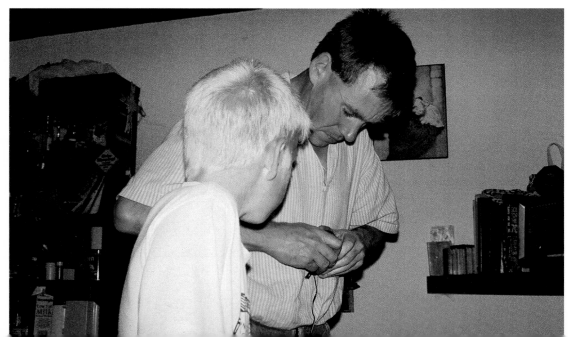

After a long day, Brian's father relaxes by taking a leisurely stroll outdoors.

Sundays with Apples, Irish Music, and Outings

An old apple tree blossoms every spring near the Lawlor family barn. In autumn, it is Brian's job to climb up where the branches are thick with apples and toss ripe ones down to his sister. Then his mother makes a delicious apple tart for Sunday dinner, which they usually have after church, in the middle of the day.

With so many apples in their tree, it takes Brian only a few minutes to pick enough for an apple tart.

Brian sets the table and practices his accordion by the fire while he waits for dinner. When Siobhan wants to practice her dancing, Brian plays the tin whistle, called a *fead°g* in Irish. Siobhan can keep up with him now, even when he plays fairly fast. Their father reads the paper and keeps time with his foot, glancing now and then at Siobhan's fancy footwork. After Sunday dinner, Brian and his family go for a drive in the country. They pass along miles of country lanes arched over with trees until they get to the rolling green hills overlooking Lough Derg.

To be a good musician for the Christian Brothers School Band requires daily practice.

There is always something interesting happening on Lough Derg. Here, the Lawlor family's attention is captured by a new jet ski in the distance.

Lough (pronounced LOCK) means "lake" in Irish, but Lough Derg is so long it almost seems like a very wide river. Pleasure boats travel up and down its length all summer long. Brian and his father admire the old barges with their fresh paint and then stop to watch a much newer way to get around on the water — a jet ski. This one can really move!

Siobhan wishes she could go swimming, but she didn't bring a bathing suit. So she hunts for berries instead and finds ripe blackberries growing wild along the fences above Lough Derg. The weather changes from sunny to cloudy to sudden rain and then back to sunny again, so the family jumps in and out of the car, dodging raindrops and stopping to walk in different scenic places whenever the sun comes out.

Old boats on Lough Derg come in a great variety of styles and designs.

With its mild and rainy climate, berries grow plentifully throughout Ireland. Siobhan soon has more than she can carry.

Ireland is often called the Emerald Isle because of its beautiful green pastures. Even on a stormy day, a hint of sun shines on the shore of Lough Derg.

Visiting Grandparents in the Irish Capital of Dublin

When Brian and Siobhan visit their grandparents in Dublin, they have a chance to see their city cousins, too. Since their grandfather, Oliver Healy, retired, he and his wife, Nora, have moved to the capital city, where four of their nine grown children live. Brian brings his inflatable world ball so they can play a sort of mini-soccer in the backyard. Even toddler cousins like to play this game!

Grandmother Nora is a woman of many talents. In addition to being a great cook, she sews clothes for her grandchildren — and their dolls! And because she is a licensed masseuse, she can rub her family's sore muscles at the end of a hard day and make them feel like new. Grandmother Nora also makes Brian's favorite dinner, a traditional Irish stew with mutton, or lamb, a dish that the Irish eat frequently.

Devout Catholics, the Healys go to church several times a week. For exercise, they ride their bicycles to church in good weather, squeezing past the cars in the driveway to unlock the front gate.

Brian's grandfather, Oliver Healy, often laughs at the playful antics of his several grandchildren. He and Grandmother Nora enjoy Brian's and Siobhan's visits. ▶

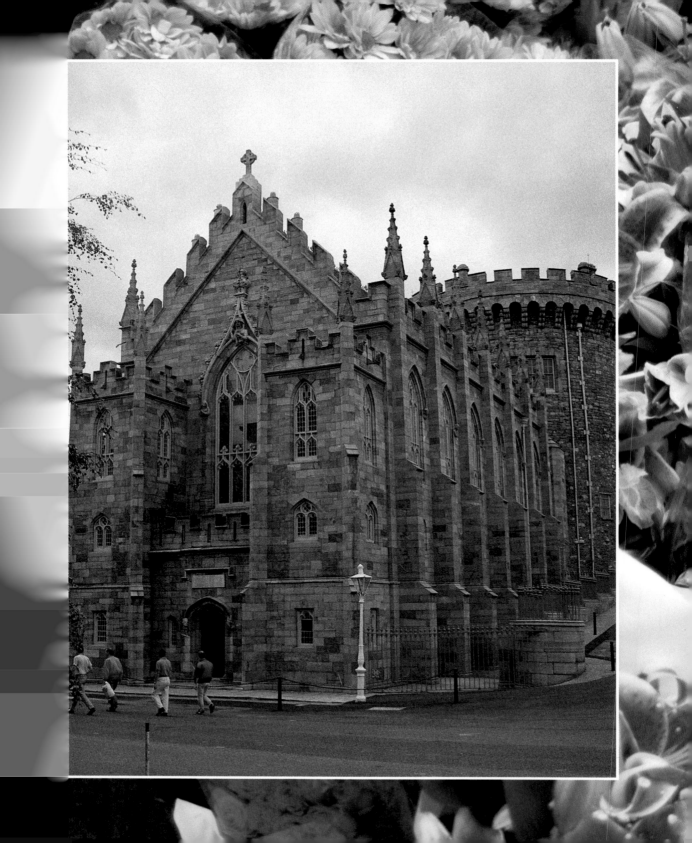

Dublin is the capital of Ireland. Brian and Siobhan can spend all day sightseeing with their grandparents and still not be finished with all there is to learn. They walk past Dublin Castle, built by the English at the order of King Henry II to defend the city and keep it under British control. The main entrance, Nora reminds her grandchildren, stands where the heads of rebellious Irish chiefs used to be displayed on spikes. This was how the British warned the Irish to accept English rule.

Literature is so important to the Irish that Dubliners put copper footprints in their sidewalks to show tourists the streets of author James Joyce. Brian follows Joyce's steps and soon they are near Trinity College. "You must see the Book of Kells!" his grandmother exclaims. This is one of the most famous and especially beautiful of medieval manuscripts. She eagerly leads everyone into Trinity College to see the wonderful book.

If you don't know where to go in Dublin, these copper footprints can lead you on a wonderful literary tour.

◀ The British built Dublin Castle in 1205 because Irish mountain clans kept attacking the English who had settled in their country. Over seven hundred years later, in 1922, the British finally gave the castle to the Irish government.

For pedestrians only, the famous Ha'penny Bridge across Dublin's River Liffey is called this because people once had to pay half a penny to cross it.

Dublin Cousins and Irish Dance

Grandmother Nora comes from quite a large family. Some of her brothers and sisters live in the United States and Canada, while others are right in Dublin. Her youngest sister, Joan, has daughters around Brian's age, named Nuala (NOO-lah) and Neasa (NAH-sah).

Brian's relatives are talented musicians and dancers, helping to keep Gaelic culture alive in modern times. Pictured here are his uncle Seamus (above) and cousin Neasa (left).

For longer trips around town, Brian's grandparents take advantage of the senior citizen discount for bus rides. But bicycles are their favorite form of transportation.

Like Siobhan, Neasa studies Irish dancing. She has competed internationally and won many medals. Her mother hand-embroiders ancient Celtic symbols onto the dresses Neasa wears in competition. Neasa's father, Seamus (SHAY-mus), plays an Irish drum called the *bohran* (Bow-RUN), and Nuala plays the flute while Neasa practices.

Nuala, Neasa, Brian, and Siobhan all like to tell Nora the Dublin slang that they know, because they can count on it to make her laugh. Dubliners like to make up rhymes for words and use them instead of the originals. For example, a wife is "trouble and strife," a telephone is a "dog and bone," a taxi is "Joe Maxi," a paycheck is a "chicken's neck," and gas in a car is "juice in a jam jar."

Homework Is Worth the Effort

During schooltime, Brian and Siobhan both have lots of homework. Last year Brian got very good grades on his report card, but he knows that he will have to continue to study just as hard this year if he wants to get good marks again. So every night, he and Siobhan sit down at the dining room table and bring out their books. It is a chance to talk over the day with their parents and ask them questions when the assignments are difficult.

Brian has to read his assignments carefully each night to be ready for his teacher's questions in class the next day.

Brian imagines a world where people can get along with one another peacefully and enjoy the beauty of the earth without polluting it.

Brian is not sure what he would like to be when he grows up, but he knows he wants to travel, see the world, and make enough money to raise a family. He knows working hard now at school will help make these plans a reality when he gets older. He loves sports and music and practices daily so that his body is strong and his musical skills are sharp. He realizes he has to exercise his mind, too, in order to be ready for his future.

FOR YOUR INFORMATION: Ireland

Official Name: Republic of Ireland (Eire)

Capital: Dublin

History

Ireland's Early Inhabitants

Irish history began after the last ice age ended. In about 7000 BC, wandering bands of hunters and gatherers moved to Ireland from Britain and the European mainland. These settlers roamed the island in search of game and, eventually, good farmland. In about 2000 BC, during the Bronze Age, people began to use bronze for tools and weapons. Beautiful decorations on their jewelry, pottery, and burial stones show that they had artistic skill and strong religious beliefs.

Even in the heart of busy Dublin, Catholics often stop for a quiet moment of prayer in the middle of the day.

The Celtic Invasion

In about 300 BC, the Celts came to Ireland from Gaul, or France. The Celts were great warriors, famous for their use of chariots in battle. They had iron swords that were stronger than bronze, so they easily took over the island and settled there.

The Celts' Gaelic language spread throughout the land. They did not have a system of writing, so their poetry and laws were chanted from one generation to the next. The Celts set up kings or chieftains to rule various areas of Ireland. Each king was assisted by councillors known as *brehons*, who were experts on laws and customs. Learned men and priests called *druids* were in charge of rituals and religious ceremonies.

Saint Patrick and the Age of Missionaries

The boy who became Saint Patrick was born in Britain around AD 390. When he was about 15 years old, an Irish raiding party captured him and other Christians and brought them back to northern Ireland as slaves. After six years, he escaped and then studied in France to be a priest.

In about 432, Patrick returned to Ireland to convert the Irish people to Christianity. He also brought literacy to the people, teaching them to read and study the Bible. Most of the Irish became Christian, and the people built monasteries where monks developed a written language for Gaelic. These monasteries were famous not just for the scholarship and learning of their monks, but also for their great libraries and many beautiful books.

Viking Invasions

In 795, the Vikings invaded Ireland in swift ships from the countries we now call Norway, Denmark, and Sweden. At first they stole cattle and valuables from the people and the rich monasteries. Then they began to raid and kill before they finally went home. But their homelands were crowded, so they began to build cities all along the Irish seacoast. By AD 1000, the Vikings were well established in Ireland.

The Gaelic kings were not strong enough to defeat the Vikings. But in the year 1002, Brian Boru became High King of all Ireland. He rebuilt some of the monasteries and churches the Vikings had destroyed and formed an army of thousands of Irishmen. On Good Friday in 1014, his army slew 7,000 Vikings at Clontarf, on the edge of Dublin. After this Battle of Brian, or Battle of Clontarf, many Vikings went home. Those who stayed became

Christians. Their families gradually intermarried with the native Irish and began to speak Gaelic.

Norman Invasions

In 1066, the Normans from France invaded and conquered England. By the late 1160s, they had attacked Ireland. In 1169, a Norman earl called Strongbow came to Ireland and declared himself king of the province of Leinster. Soon many other Norman noblemen came with soldiers who wore armor and brought crossbows, longbows, giant catapults, and battering rams to smash the Irish fortresses. The Irish soldiers had only swords and spears and no armor, so the Normans easily took control of Irish lands. In 1171, Henry II, the Norman king of England, declared himself king of Ireland, too.

English Domination and Catholic Persecution

For centuries, the English let the Irish govern themselves as long as they recognized the English king as their ruler. But in 1541, King Henry VIII of England began to confiscate Irish lands and monasteries. Henry had left the Catholic Church so that he could divorce his first wife, Catherine, and remarry in the hopes of having a son. Catherine had managed so far to bear only a daughter, Mary. When he left the Roman Catholic Church, most of England left with him and became Protestant.

Henry's daughter Mary became queen in 1553. She began a program called "plantation," which evicted the Irish from their lands and replaced them with "planted" English settlers or Irish who were loyal to England. Mary's sister, Elizabeth I, became England's queen in 1558. Elizabeth I ordered the Irish to become Protestant, too. She sentenced Catholic priests to death and outlawed Catholic religious services.

Elizabeth's successor, James I, "planted" Scottish and English Protestants in place of Catholics in the northern part of Ireland. To this day, this part of Ireland remains part of the United Kingdom.

The Oppressor and "The Great Liberator"

Oliver Cromwell ruled England from 1649 to 1658, and he slaughtered thousands of Irish who tried to revolt against the English Parliament. The population of Ireland dropped from about 1.5 million to less than 1 million during that time because so many had been killed or had fled the country. By the late 1600s, more than 85% of Irish lands were in English hands.

The English established penal laws that punished people for practicing Catholicism. Catholics were not allowed to vote, hold public office, or own property, a gun, or a horse worth more than five pounds. They were not allowed to become lawyers or teachers, and Catholic schools were outlawed. Some Irish children attended Protestant schools, and some went to Irish colleges in Europe, but many didn't go to school at all. The Catholic Irish did not regain the right to vote until 1793.

England, Scotland, and Ireland formally merged in 1801 to form the United Kingdom. In 1828, the Irish elected Daniel O'Connell, who had long fought for Catholic rights, to represent them in British Parliament. The British were afraid to deny O'Connell his seat because they thought the Irish would rebel. So they created the Catholic Emancipation Act of 1829, which granted Catholics the right to be members of British Parliament. To this day, Daniel O'Connell is known as the "Liberator" because he forced the British to give Ireland some political power through legal means.

The Great Hunger

In 1845, much of the Irish population of eight million was largely dependent on the potato as their main food. Between 1845 and 1847, a disease called potato blight infected the potatoes. The Irish had nothing to eat. The British government helped a little, but over a million Irish people starved to death. Another 1.6 million emigrated to the United States and Great Britain to escape "The Great Hunger." By 1851, the population of Ireland was down from 8 million to 5.5 million.

The Fight For Independence Continues

Inspired by the example and achievements of O'Connell, the Irish began a series of movements to gain Home Rule — that is, to have the power to decide their own local affairs while Britain handled international disputes for them. The Home Rule Association was founded by Isaac Butt and began to work for legal independence from England. In 1858, the Irish Republican Brotherhood in Ireland and Britain also started to push for freedom. The members even began a secret society in the United States called the Fenian Brotherhood, which soon became an international organization.

Under the leadership of Charles Stuart Parnell, the Irish members of Parliament almost won Home Rule in 1886. The Irish Protestant Parnell had been elected to the British Parliament in 1875. But the Home Rule bills of 1886 and 1892 did not pass, largely because of Ireland's Protestants. They preferred British rule to the possibility of having the Irish Catholic majority dominate them. A third attempt in 1912-14 led Parliament to pass a Home Rule bill, but it was suspended by the outbreak of World War I.

Rebellions and Revolutions

The Sinn Féin Society (Gaelic for "We Ourselves") was founded in 1905. The members wanted Ireland to stop electing people to the British Parliament and, instead, set up its own government in Ireland.

In 1916, a leader of the Irish Republican Brotherhood, Padraic Pearse, and other revolutionaries led an armed revolt. On April 24, the day after Easter Sunday, Pearse and his troops seized buildings and declared "the right of the people of Ireland to the ownership of Ireland," and proclaimed the Irish Republic "a sovereign independent state" that "guarantees religious and civil liberty, equal rights, and equal opportunities to all its citizens." The Easter Rising failed after a week of bloody battles. Padraic Pearse and the other leaders were executed.

Two years later, the Sinn Féin lawmakers elected by the Irish refused to go to the British Parliament. Instead, they formed the *Dáil Eéireann*, or Irish House of Deputies, in Dublin. On January 21, 1919, they officially declared the Independent Republic of Ireland that Padraic Pearse had proclaimed in the Easter Rising. That same year, the Irish Republican Army (IRA) was formed to fight for recognition of Ireland's independence from Britain. Michael Collins led IRA raids on the British-controlled Irish police. The British government then formed the Black and Tans, a special police force that fought in the streets with the IRA.

In 1920, the British Parliament tried to solve the problem by passing the Government of Ireland Act, which divided Ireland into two self-governing sections. They kept Northern Ireland as part of the United Kingdom. Most of the people in Northern Ireland accepted the act, but the other 26 counties refused it because it would maintain British Parliamentary control.

The IRA continued to fight the Black and Tans until a truce was arranged in July 1921. After five months of negotiation, the Anglo-Irish Treaty of 1921 created the Irish Free State, consisting of the island's 26 southern counties. However, this treaty still left Northern Ireland in the British Empire. Plus, English naval bases could remain in Irish ports, and the Irish Free State had to call the English monarch their chief of state.

Sinn Féin and the IRA had differing feelings about the treaty. But the majority in both accepted it and became part of the government and army of the Irish Free State. The minority IRA continued to fight those who supported the treaty. This led to the Irish Civil War (1922-23), in which at least 500 people died before the antitreaty forces were defeated.

Toward Complete Independence

Eamon de Valera served as president of the Executive Committee of the Irish Free State from 1932 until 1937. He cut ties with Great Britain by abolishing the oath of allegiance to the king and by helping to create a new constitution under which the country was to be ruled by a president and a prime minister. But it wasn't until 1948 that the Irish Free State became completely independent for the first time in seven centuries. Irish lawmakers changed the name of their country to the Republic of Ireland and officially left the British Commonwealth.

In the 1960s, Catholics in Northern Ireland formed civil rights groups to combat what they saw as social and economic discrimination against them by the Protestants. Riots in Belfast and Londonderry between the Catholics and the Protestants brought British troops in 1969 to keep the peace. This tense political situation characterized Northern Ireland throughout the 1970s and 1980s and exists to this day. The modern IRA continues to fight for a united independent Ireland, while the Protestants continue to resist.

Government

The Republic of Ireland is a parliamentary democracy led by a prime minister and the Parliament. The prime minister is elected by the Parliament and is usually the leader of the strongest political group at the time. Citizens elect a president to a seven-year term, and he or she may not serve more than two terms. This is largely a ceremonial office. The president presents other officials with their seals of office, accepts the credentials of foreign diplomats, and represents the country on state visits abroad.

The Parliament consists of 166 elected members of the Irish House of Deputies and 60 members of the Senate. Some members of the Senate are appointed by the prime minister and some are elected. The Irish also elect 15 members to the European Parliament.

Judges are appointed by the prime minister and serve for life unless impeached by both houses of Parliament. Ireland's court system is divided into district (local) and circuit (regional) courts. Serious crimes, like murder, treason, and piracy, are tried in criminal courts. The highest court in Ireland is the Supreme Court.

The Republic of Ireland consists of 26 counties, each with its own locally elected government. The Republic is now totally independent of Great Britain and is an independent member of the United Nations and European Community. The legal voting age in the Republic of Ireland is 18.

Education

Ireland places great importance on education. Schools are free, and attendance is required of everyone between the ages of six and fifteen. Primary schools (grades 1-9) are state-funded but run mostly by either Catholic or Protestant religious groups. Secondary schools (grades 10-12) are privately owned, but they are also run by religious groups. There are also some community schools not associated with religious groups.

Vocational schools that train young people to enter skilled occupations are financed partly by local authorities and partly by the state. Students from all secondary schools must take state examinations by age 16 to get their Intermediate Certificate and again two years later to receive their Leaving Certificate. Their scores determine their qualification for higher education.

In addition to nine vocational schools and five colleges for training teachers, there are four universities, two being Trinity College in Dublin, founded in 1591, and the National University of Ireland, founded in 1909.

Currency

The Irish pound or *punt* is the official currency of the Republic of Ireland. In 1992, one Irish pound equalled $1.65 in US money and $2.00 in Canadian. There are 100 pence, or pennies, in a *punt*. Unlike many nations that feature political figures on their bills, Ireland features great writers and famous figures from mythology. Coins display an Irish harp on one side and an animal on the other.

Beautiful Gaelic writing and Celtic symbols decorate modern Irish money.

Population and Ethnic Groups

The vast majority, some 97% of the population of the Republic of Ireland, are descendants of early Irish tribes who intermarried with invading Celts,

Vikings, and Normans. The remaining Irish are primarily descendants of English, French, and Scottish Protestants who settled on the island in the 16th and 17th centuries.

Language

For centuries, the people of Ireland spoke Gaelic, or Irish, an ancient Celtic language closely related to Welsh. However, the British discouraged its use and began to replace it with English in the 16th century. By 1900, only a few people in the far west of Ireland still spoke Gaelic, and despite efforts to revive it, Gaelic has almost completely died out as a spoken language. As it stands, the majority of the Irish today speak English as their first language. But to preserve Gaelic as part of the Irish heritage, the government has made it one of the official languages of Ireland; English is the official second language. The Gaelic League, founded in 1893, helps to preserve and revive Irish language, legends, history, music, and dance. Gaelic is taught daily in all the primary schools, and all public signs and government documents must be printed in both English and Gaelic.

Land and Climate

The Republic of Ireland covers five-sixths of the island of Ireland as well as several small neighboring islands. At 27,136 square miles (70,283 sq km) in area, it is the same size as the Canadian province of New Brunswick and slightly larger than the US state of West Virginia. At its widest point east to west, it is 177 miles (285 km), while its greatest distance north to south is 289 miles (465 km).

Ireland's landscape consists of seacoasts, mountain ranges, and a central plain that is largely farmland. This includes the peat bogs that provide fuel for home fires and green pastures. The highest mountain is Carrantuohill in the Macgillycuddy's Reeks range in the southwest. Ireland has many lakes, called *loughs*, primarily in the central plains. The lakes of Killarney in county Kerry are especially beautiful and attract many tourists. The longest river is the Shannon, which connects several lakes to the Atlantic Ocean.

Because it lies in the path of the Gulf Stream, Ireland's climate is mild, and snow is rare. Winter temperatures rarely fall below 40°F (4°C), and summer temperatures average 60°F (16°C). Rain falls on all or part of 200 days in some parts of the island. The west coast averages from 40 inches (100 cm) to 100 inches (250 cm) of rain per year. Eastern Ireland escapes with somewhat less, but it still rains there about every other day.

IRELAND – Political and Physical

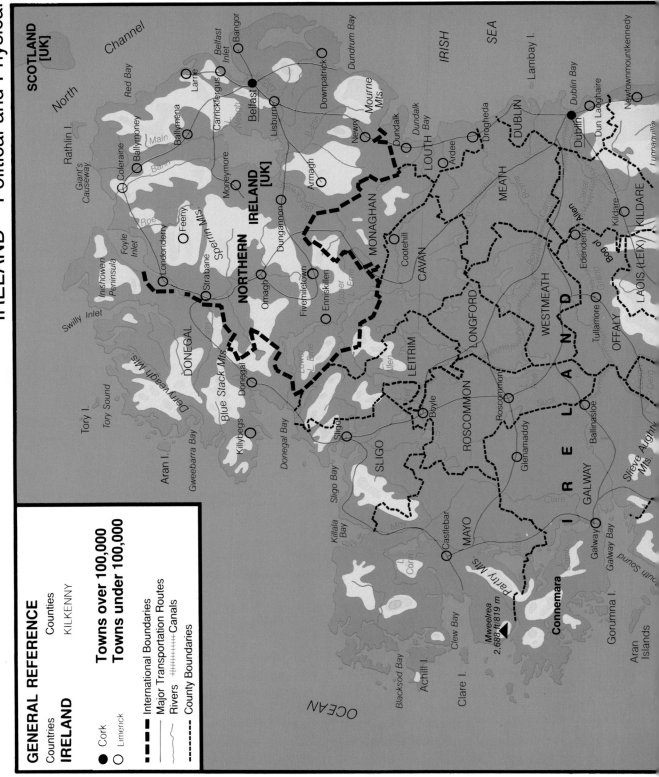

GENERAL REFERENCE

Countries   Counties
IRELAND   KILKENNY

● Cork   **Towns over 100,000**
○ Limerick   **Towns under 100,000**

▪▪▪▪▪ International Boundaries
──── Major Transportation Routes
∿∿∿ Rivers ++++++Canals
┄┄┄┄ County Boundaries

SCOTLAND
[UK]

North
Channel

Red Bay
Rathlin I.
Giant's Causeway

Larne
Belfast Inlet
Carrickfergus
Bangor
Belfast
Lisburn
Downpatrick
Dundrum Bay

Ballymoney
Ballymena
Coleraine
Moneymore
Main
Bann

Mourne Mts.
Newry
Dundalk
Dundalk Bay
Ardee
LOUTH

Armagh
MONAGHAN
Cootehill
CAVAN

IRISH
SEA

Lambay I.
Drogheda
DUBLIN
Dublin
Dublin Bay
Dun Laoghaire
Newtownmountkennedy

Foyle Inlet
Inishowen Peninsula
Feeny
Londonderry
Strabane
Sperrin Mts.
Roe

NORTHERN
IRELAND
[UK]

Dungannon
Omagh
Fivemiletown
Enniskillen
Upper L. Erne
Lower L. Erne

MEATH
Boyne
Royal Canal
Edenderry
Bog of Allen
Kildare
KILDARE
LAOIS (LEIX)
Luggnaquilla

WESTMEATH
LONGFORD
LEITRIM
L. Allen
Tullamore
OFFALY
Grand Canal

Swilly Inlet
DONEGAL
Derryveagh Mts.
Tory Sound
Tory I.

Blue Stack Mts.
Donegal
Killybegs
Donegal Bay

Sligo
SLIGO
Sligo Bay
Boyle
ROSCOMMON
Roscommon
Suck
Shannon

Aran I.
Gweebarra Bay

Killala Bay
Castlebar
MAYO
L. Corrib
Partry Mts.

Ballinasloe
Glenamaddy
GALWAY
Galway
Galway Bay
Slieve Aughty Mts.
Deel

Blacksod Bay
Achill I.
Clew Bay
Clare I.

Mweelrea
2,688 ft/819 m
Connemara
Gorumna I.
Aran Islands
South Sound

OCEAN

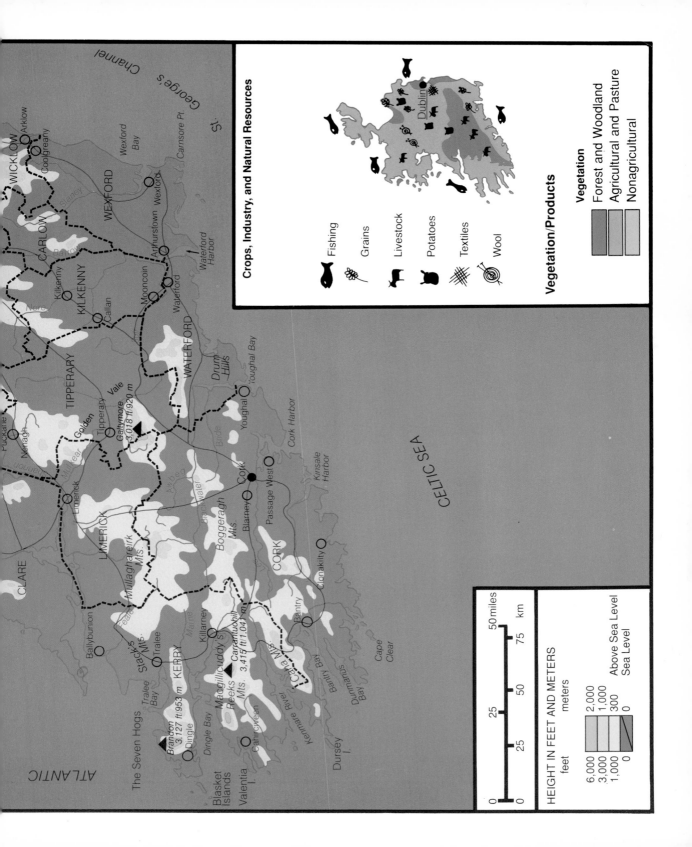

Crops, Industry, and Natural Resources

Fishing

Grains

Livestock

Potatoes

Textiles

Wool

Vegetation/Products

Vegetation

Forest and Woodland

Agricultural and Pasture

Nonagricultural

HEIGHT IN FEET AND METERS

feet   meters

6,000   2,000
3,000   1,000
1,000   300   Above Sea Level
    0   0   Sea Level

0   25   50   75   km

0   25   50 miles

ATLANTIC

The Seven Hogs

Brandon 3,127 ft/953 m

Dingle

Tralee Bay

Stack's Mts.

KERRY

Blasket Islands

Valentia I.

Cahirciveen

Macgillicuddy's Reeks 3,415 ft/1,041 m

Killarney

Tralee

Carrauntoohill

Caha Mts.

Kenmare River

Dursey I.

Bantry Bay

Dunmanus Bay

Cape Clear

Ballybunion

Mullaghareirk Mts.

Maine

Blackwater

Bantry

Clonakility

CORK

Boggeragh Mts.

Blarney

Passage West

Kinsale Harbor

CELTIC SEA

Cork

Cork Harbor

Youghal

Youghal Bay

Bride

Drum Hills

WATERFORD

Waterford Harbor

Waterford

Mooncoin

Callan

Nore

KILKENNY

Kilkenny

CARLOW

Barrow

WEXFORD

Arthurstown

Wexford

Carnsore Pt.

Wexford Bay

Slaney

WICKLOW

Arklow

Coolgreany

George's Channel

St. George's Channel

CLARE

LIMERICK

Limerick

Shannon

Nenagh

Puckane

Mullear

TIPPERARY

Golden

Tipperary

Vale

Galtymore 3,018 ft/920 m

Suir

Anner

Celtic Sea

Natural Resources, Agriculture, and Industry

Ireland is known as the Emerald Isle because the high rainfall and moderate temperatures make its grass some of the greenest in the world, perfect for grazing cattle, sheep, and horses. About two-thirds of the nation is farmland, most of it pasture. Cattle and beef products account for about half of Ireland's agricultural output and are the country's main export. The wool from Irish sheep is world-famous for its quality. In addition to dairy farms and other livestock raising, Irish farmers grow potatoes, oats, barley, wheat, turnips, and sugar beets. Ireland also has a worldwide reputation for breeding fine racehorses.

About a third of the labor force works in industry. Irish industries have a hard time surviving in the European market because of competition from huge industrial powers like Britain, Germany, and France. Most industries are privately owned, but the government controls some oil refineries, as well as some shipbuilding and fertilizer companies. Unfortunately, unemployment in Ireland is the worst in Western Europe.

Perhaps Ireland's most profitable source of income is tourism. Two to three million visitors arrive each year from around the world; sometimes there are as many tourists as native Irish. Some travelers come to trace the footsteps of their favorite authors or literary characters. Others visit their ancestral homes, search for famous places in Irish history, or gaze at the lush countryside.

Art and Culture

The ancient Irish preferred to tell stories rather than write them down.

The Gaelic word for telephone is close enough to English to need no translation on this country phone booth in Puckane.

This storytelling tradition produced folktales and legends of banshees, leprechauns, saints, and heroes still known the world over. Ireland is the birthplace of many famous writers, such as Jonathan Swift, Oscar Wilde, and James Joyce.

Ireland also has a long history of fine art, as the many carved crosses and decorated manuscripts indicate. The Book of Kells, an eighth-century bible, has beautiful, elaborate designs on every page. People today can also enjoy old Celtic styles, as most modern jewelry in Ireland recreates the art of the ancient Celts. Modern Irish artists include painters Jack Yeats and John Keating, and Irish music and dance are experiencing a revival as young people study and perform ancient melodies and the lively dances that go with them. Groups like The Chieftains help keep traditional music alive, while many folk groups use Irish harps and melodies. Modern rock music also thrives in Ireland, which is the home of musicians Bob Geldof, Sinead O'Connor, and the group U2.

Sports and Recreation

The Irish love sports of all kinds. The ancient sports of Gaelic football and hurling remain the most popular games in Ireland today. Gaelic football combines elements of soccer and rugby, while hurling resembles field hockey. The All-Ireland Hurling Championship, held each September, often draws a crowd of more than 80,000 people. Soccer, an international sport, is also followed closely and played in fierce competition. Other popular sports include boating, swimming, golf, tennis, bicycling, jogging, boxing, and horseback riding.

Irish horses are internationally known for speed and beauty. They compete in races at more than two dozen tracks in Ireland. The best-known Irish races, the Irish Derby and the Irish Grand National, are celebrated almost as if they were national holidays.

Religion

The Republic of Ireland is about 94% Roman Catholic, while most of the Protestant minority belong to the Anglican, Episcopalian, Presbyterian, and Methodist churches. Religious groups play a large role in the education process, and priests have traditionally been important members of their communities. Irish Catholics have many churches and frequently go on pilgrimages to monasteries, shrines, and holy places such as Croagh Patrick in County Mayo, where Saint Patrick prayed and fasted for the 40 days of Lent in the year 441.

The Book of Kells, an eighth-century bible, is a graceful, imaginative work of art. Many of its beautiful images are reproduced on postcards and posters for everyone to enjoy.

Dublin

Dublin, a thriving city of over 650,000 people, is the capital of Ireland. In addition to housing the government, it is the nation's business, educational, and cultural center. Dublin began when the Vikings turned the village of Dubh Linn (Gaelic for "black pool") into a seaport and trading town over 1,000 years ago. Sometimes called "the largest small town in the world," it has few tall buildings and no skyscrapers. The city buildings span architectural styles from many time periods and include modern buildings as well. Among its landmarks are Phoenix Park, the General Post Office, and Trinity College. The River Liffey divides the city into northern and southern halves and is spanned by many bridges. Dublin is still an elegant city despite the damage it suffered during the Easter Rising, the revolution, and the civil war, when several fine landmarks were destroyed by bombardments and shootouts.

Irish in North America

So many people left Ireland in the great migration of the 1840s that there are now more people of Irish descent in other countries than there are in Ireland. In the United States alone, there are about 40 million people of Irish descent — roughly ten times the total population of the Republic of Ireland! Canada has approximately 3.5 million people of Irish origin.

More Books about Ireland

The Easter Rising. Grant (Franklin Watts)
Ireland. Pomeray (Chelsea House)
Land of Tales: Stories of Ireland for Children. Ryan and Snell
    (Irish Books Media)
The Republic of Ireland. Fradin (Childrens Press)
See Inside a Castle. Unstead (Warwick Press)
Shamrocks, Harps, and Shillelaghs. Barth (Houghton, Mifflin)
Tim O'Toole and the Wee Folk. McDurmott (Viking Press)
We Live in Ireland. Fairclough (Bookwright Press)

Glossary of Important Terms

banshee............a wailing female spirit or ghost in old Gaelic stories.

Gaelic ....the language spoken by the Celts who settled in Ireland 2,500 years ago. Although little-spoken today, it is one of the two official languages of the Republic of Ireland.

hurling..............an ancient Irish sport similar to field hockey. Players divide into two teams that score goals by hitting the ball with curved sticks to drive it into nets on opposite sides of the playing field.

leprechaun ....a mischievous elf in Irish stories and myths, thought to guard over hidden treasure.

medieval...........anything having to do with the Middle Ages, the period between the fall of the Roman Empire in the fifth century and the revival of Western culture in the 15th century.

Glossary of Useful Gaelic (Irish) Terms

baile (BAH-luh).....................................home
buachaill (BOO-ah-chel).......................boy
cailín (CUHL-een)................................ girl
ceol (QUOLE)......................................music
daidí (DAD-ee)....................................father
mamaí (MAM-ee)...............................mother
obair (UHB-er)....................................work
scoil (SKOYL).......................................school
súgradh (SOO-gruh)............................play

Things to Do — Research Projects and Activities

Mainly because of its ongoing political struggles, Ireland is almost always an active part of international news. Many Irish people are working very hard to solve the problems that come with the island's division, in the hope that there will one day be peaceful Irish unity.

The following research projects might help you understand some of the important issues in Ireland. For accurate, up-to-date information, you may have to go to the nearest library. Ask for one or both of the following publications, which will have listings of recent articles on many topics. Look up *Ireland* in these two publications:

Readers' Guide to Periodical Literature
Children's Magazine Guide

1. Irish children grow up with ancient castles in their towns and nearby countryside. Research how some of these castles looked and then make a castle to scale from cardboard or other suitable material.

2. Millions of Irish came to the US and Canada during the 1840s and after to escape famine and oppression at home. Contact the local historical society to find out if any came to your area. If so, what did they contribute to your hometown? Are there any traces of their presence remaining today?

3. Find a book with pictures of ancient Celtic art. See if you can use Celtic designs to create your own poster.

4. Listen to recorded Irish music, such as the Chieftains or James Galway's flute music. Then buy a tin whistle from your local music shop and see if you can pick out an Irish tune.

5. If you would like a pen pal in Ireland, write to either of these two groups:

International Pen Friends
P.O. Box 290065
Brooklyn, NY 11229

Worldwide Pen Friends
P.O. Box 39097
Downey, CA 90241

Be sure to tell them what country you want your pen pal to be from. Also include your full name, age, and address.

Index

DATE DUE

FEB 1 4 1994 (4)			
MAR 3 1 1994 (6)			
5-23-95 (4)			
BURRELL			
MAY 0 1 1996 (4)			
Burrell			
APR 2 5 1997 (4)			
12/14/98			
10/28/99			
2/6/01			
DEC 1 4 2001			